and
Knife Making

by Jim Watson

Schiffer
Publishing Ltd

West Chester, Pennsylvania 19380

Y0-AAP-119

Dedication

This book is dedicated, as are all my successes, to my wife Sylvia and my son Jamie. I may make the living in the family but Sylvia makes life worth living, she has been my support for the past twenty-three years.

Edited by Lyngerda Kelley.
Printed in the United States of America.
ISBN: 0-88740-118-X
Published by Schiffer Publishing Ltd.
1469 Morstein Road, West Chester, Pennsylvania 19380

This book may be purchased from the publisher.
Please include $2.00 postage.
Try your bookstore first.

Contents

Acknowledgements

A special thank you goes to my friends and fellow members of the Charlotte Woodcarving Club, who have always been a help to me. The comradeship and fellowship I have found there is very special. I also want to thank Tom and Nancy Wolfe for introducing me to the Schiffer Publishing team, Peter and Nancy Shiffer and Lyn Kelley. They made an old country boy like me feel right at home with Southern hospitality Northern style. Most of all I must thank God. I prayed to him about taking on a project like this and it is through his guidance that it became a reality.

Preface

Before you begin to learn how to sharpen tools and make knives the Jim Watson way, there are two words which must be taken to heart, *practice* and *patience*. This he illustrates with a little story.

"A buddy of mine was planning his first trip to the big apple, New York City. Naturally one of the most important sights to see was Carnegie Hall. After he got to New York he began to look around the city and take in all there is to see. In his travels he stopped a passerby on the street and asked him if he could tell him how to get to Carnegie Hall. The passerby responded, 'Practice, practice, practice.' "

To really sharpen tools the right way and do a good job, these are the two essential ingredients—practice and patience. It is most important to learn by hand the traditional way so you know what you are looking for and can see what you want. Once this technique is mastered, going on with the aid of power tools is the next step. "You can mess up a lot faster with a power tool than when you are working by hand."

Jim's method of sharpening was taught to him by his granddad, he offers it only as a suggested way to successfully sharpen tools and knives. If you are currently using a method you are happy with and achieving results to your satisfaction, then realize that this is just another way to achieve those results and you may or may not choose to incorporate these techniques.

However, if you think that maybe you can get just a little better cutting edge and, as a result, an improved carving with a cleaner cut, then give these ideas a try. Most people will begin to use a tool when it is sharp, Jim shows how to go the extra step and hone and polish that tool to achieve and maintain the best possible results and a superior edge.

"You can always cut with something sharp but you cannot necessarily carve with it."

Making this extra effort to achieve the best possible cutting edge naturally does require patience and practice, which also reminded Jim of a story:

"This old man about sixty or so got married to an eighteen year old girl. They hadn't been married long when the young girl went to town to do some shopping. She came home to find the old man in bed with a sixty year old woman. The young girl was understandably very upset and asked the old man what a sixty year old woman had that an eighteen year old didn't. The old man smiled and replied gently, 'Patience.' "

Introduction

Anyone who has ever experienced the frustrations of trying to cut or carve with a dull tool will appreciate the need to be able to properly sharpen that tool. To achieve good quality work and ease in the process, sharp, well maintained tools are essential. The time invested in sharpening is small when compared to the feeling of satisfaction achieved when using a well sharpened, honed and polished tool.

When tools are purchased they have already been ground and sharpened to a factory ground edge. This should be given the really fine edge that comes with the final honing and polishing process. The various methods depend upon the type of tool.

This book will illustrate the sharpening process for wood carving tools and knives of various sizes and shapes, also pocket knives and kitchen knives. The materials necessary for sharpening will be discussed as well as methods for reconditioning knives, and tools and resurfacing the sharpening stones. By following these instructions with a little practice and patience, anyone will be able to obtain an edge as keen as the piece of steel will allow.

The types of tools and knives you will sharpen depends upon the type of carving you do and your particular needs. The following pages give instructions on sharpening numerous different tools and knives. Every carver will be doing him/herself a favor by taking a day off now and then to sharpen tools. It saves time and work in the long run.

Generally the sharpening procedure for any tool or knife is the same, it is the technique that varies. Begin sharpening tools on a coarse sharpening stone, as the tool becomes sharp progress to a finer grit sharpening stone. These stones are used until the wire edge is achieved on the tool.

The wire edge is an indication of the end of the sharpening process. It is the very edge of the blade which has been ground so far that it bends away from the sharpening stone instead of staying rigid and being ground away. The wire edge should be carefully removed. It can be seen, especially with a magnifying glass and can also be felt. It should always be removed to ensure a good foundation for the cutting edge.

It is during the honing process that the wire edge is gently removed and the fully sharpened edge is defined. Honing is done on a piece of leather that has been covered with compound. The technique is the same as was used to sharpen the tool. Once fully honed the final step is to polish the blade to a mirror finish. The best results are achieved with the use of a polishing wheel, however a piece of leather with a fine grit compound can also be used for polishing purposes. A tool is not ready to be used until it has gone through these steps of sharpening, honing and polishing.

Tools and knives that do not have a badly damaged edge may need only to be honed and polished before being put to use. Before beginning to carve take a good look at your tools and determine their individual condition. Some may need to be sharpened and some just a quick honing and polishing. The important point to remember is that at the very minimum every tool should have a few "licks across the leather" before it is carved with.

Tools and Supplies

There are not a lot of supplies needed to properly sharpen a tool. Jim uses either Japanese water stones, or oil stones with honing oil, and a piece of leather with compound. Depending on the tool or knife to be sharpened and how dull it is, Jim will also use a grinding wheel and frequently a polishing wheel. The grinding wheel is used much more in the actual knife making process than in sharpening because it is just too easy to make serious mistakes on a grinding wheel, especially for the inexperienced. Doing the process by hand is most successful and does yield the best results. Jim also uses a work bench as a sharpening and carving table. It is important that sharpening be done on a flat stable surface, especially with water stones.

Sharpening Stones

Sharpening stones are available in two different types, oil or water stones. Both are equally as effective for sharpening, they are simply different means of achieving the same results. Which type of stone to use is a personal decision based on preference.

Arkansas stones are frequently used with oil as the lubricating agent. They can also be used with water, and come in three different grades. The grey stone is called soft Arkansas and has a medium grit. The fine grit stone is white and is called hard Arkansas. Black Arkansas is a black stone that is extra fine grit.

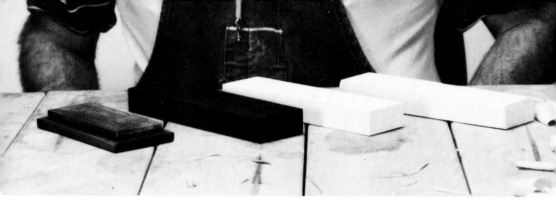

Soft Arkansas will quickly produce a sharp edge on tools or knives. Hard Arkansas is used for touch up and polishing an already sharpened edge. Black Arkansas is only used for special intricate sharpening needs or for finishing.

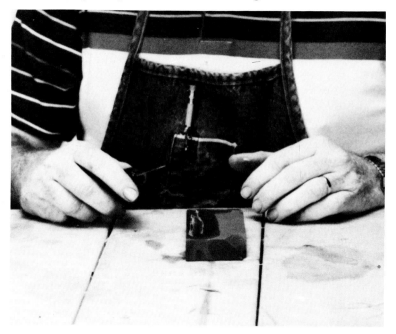

In the illustrations the stones are used with oil as a lubricant. Each stone comes individually packaged and has instructions for its use enclosed. Honing oil or light lubricating oil is used for oil stones. It is usually applied by pouring a small line along the length of the stone and then spreading the oil over the surface area to be used, making a light, thin coating. Too much oil will make the knife slide across the stone without any sharpening effect at all.

Oil stones can get saturated and clogged with oil and particles from knives. They can be cleaned with warm soapy water or with Varsol, which is brushed or rubbed on and then wiped off. The stone will feel especially slick when it is time to clean it.

Japanese Water stones are used exclusively with water as a lubricant. They should be immersed in water for five to ten minutes to enable the porous stone to fill with water. When stored the stone should be kept in a plastic container so it is ready for use at any time.

While sharpening with a water stone, be sure to periodically drip water on the surface to keep it well lubricated. Japanese Water Stones tend to wear faster than oil stones, which is also a reason that they sharpen more quickly than oil stones. Water Stones also come in a variety of different grits depending upon the sharpening need.

The sharpening process begins with a more coarse stone for the initial sharpening and then polishing and honing is done on a finer grit stone. Both water and oil stones are used the same way. The actual sharpening procedure is the same.

No matter what type of stone is used, they should be stored properly to prevent breaking or chipping. The stones can always be stored in their original boxes or a wooden box can be made to keep sharpening stones safe. A support or platform can also be made to stabilize the stone and prevent it from moving while it is being used. This can be as simple or complex as you choose to make it.

While using a water stone it should be kept in a shallow waterproof dish or plastic lid to eliminate the mess from the water. The finer the grit the more quickly it absorbs water.

Slip stones are small versions of sharpening stones and come in a variety of shapes to make sharpening small tools or intricate shapes easier. They too can be lubricated with either water or oil, depending upon the stone. Different shaped stones are used for variously shaped tools.

In all stones for sharpening, the higher the number of the stone, the finer the grit. The water stones are available in many different grits from 250 up to 8000. Coarse stones are used for sharpening and fine stones are for polishing and honing. Some oil stones are available as combination stones with a different grit on the front and back.

Polishing Wheel

The polishing wheel is used to touch up an already sharp blade or edge and to hone that mirror finish on the edges. Jim uses the *Black and Decker Polishing Wheel*, which is easy to use and portable. You can get the same results by hand as you can with a polishing wheel, but it takes a lot more time.

The polishing wheel pictured here has two sides. It has a cloth wheel and a leather wheel. Both wheels are used in the honing and polishing process. The illustrations show how each wheel is used.

The wheel should be used with compound and be sure you have a good hold of the tool before you put it against the wheel. For small gouges it will still be necessary to use the edge of a piece of leather to hone and polish such a small surface for the best results. New tools can have the finishing touch added by the polishing wheel. Learn from other sharpeners and remember to practice and take time.

Here a gouge is being honed on the leather side of the polishing wheel. The leather is well saturated with polishing compound.

The final polish is put on with the use of the cloth side of the polishing wheel. Again it has been rubbed with polishing compound.

Take care to hold the tool tightly as the momentum of the wheel can cause the tool to fly out of your grip.

Holding the tool and polishing the other side.

Leather and Compounds

Scraps of leather in varying widths and lengths make perfect honing material. An old leather belt works well also. Honing and polishing are the two final and very important steps in the sharpening process. The leather should be lubricated with either a little oil, compound or jewelers rouge. Compounds come in different colors for different grits; for the purposes here the green compound works best, especially for tools such as chisels. It is just rubbed on the leather to penetrate it before the honing and polishing is begun.

Rub the compound on the leather before honing.

Examples of lapping compound as it comes in sets of two cans of coarse and fine grit.

When honing knives, lapping compound should be used. It is usually purchased in sets of two small cans, one of coarse and one of fine grit, each having different colors. The compound adds a smoother edge and actually polishes the cutting edge.

Shown here is an easy-to-make leather stand with three pieces of leather, each with a different grade of compound, coarse, fine and medium. The different grades of compound are identified by the tacks in the end of the leather mount. Here number one is the most coarse and three the finest. Once sharpening on the stone is completed, honing and polishing on leather begins.

Jim recommends a "couple of licks" on the leather daily before you start carving, or when you are through carving at the end of the day. It will eliminate a lot of work if you never let your tools become too dull.

To test the sharpness of a tool, Jim will try to run the edge down his fingernail. If it grabs and catches you can be sure your edge is sharp. If it slides off your nail there is still more sharpening work to be done.

Applying compound to one side of the leather stand.

Tacks on the end of the leather mount, identify the grade of compound used on that side.

Honing and polishing on the leather stand.

Sharpening Your Tools

Gouges

Gouges are as important in woodcarving as knives. They are a hollowed carving tool with the cutting edge on the curve. Gouges come in a vast variety of shapes and sweeps. They are referred to as veiners, spoon gouges, back bent gouges, bent gouges, fish tail gouges, etc. Some of these types will be further discussed in the following pages and methods to sharpen them will be shown.

Gouge #8

Using an 800 grit Japanese Water Stone, rotate the edge of the gouge from side to side across the stone.

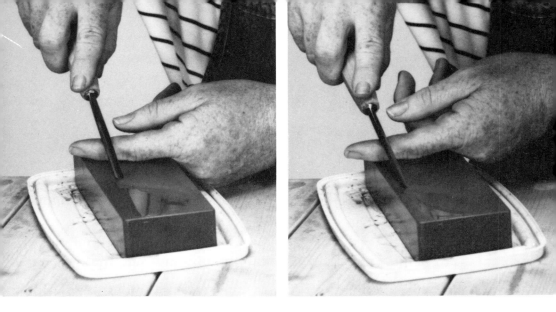

Use index finger as a guide to maintain the correct 25° angle.

Once sharpened, begin to hone on an 8000 grit water stone.

Rotate in the same motion as when sharpening.

Use a slip stone to hone the inside of the sharpened edge.

Polish on leather with compound.

Rotate the tool along the leather from side to side as was done on the stone.

Hone the inside of the gouge along the edge of a piece of leather.

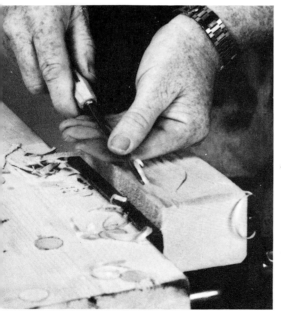 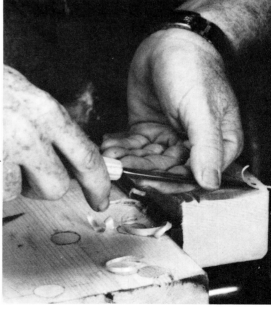

Test for sharpness and correct cutting edge on a block of wood.

The polished edge.

Gouge #7

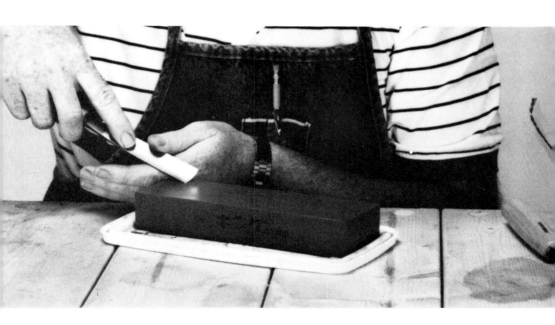

A water stone or oil stone can be used to sharpen any tool. To sharpen this gouge, a Japanese Water Stone was used. Begin on one end of the sweep.

Rotate the edge toward the other side on a 25-30° angle.

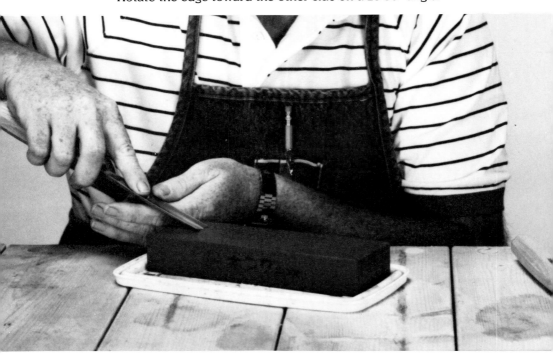

Maintain the angle while rotating the edge along the stone.

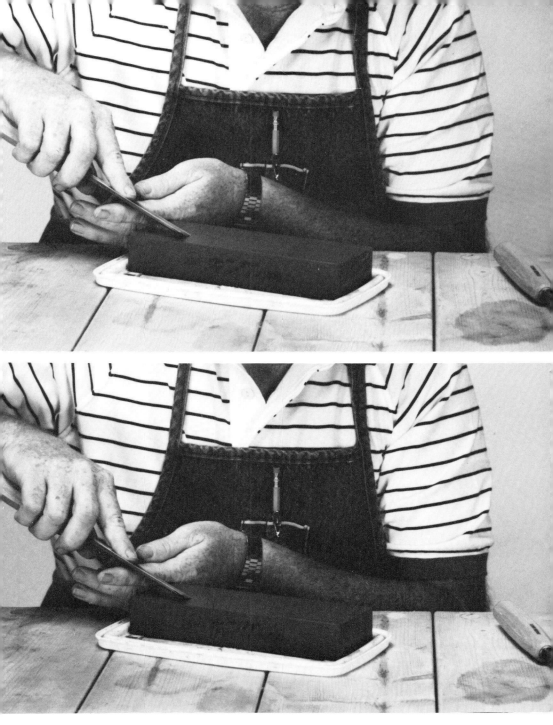

Rotate all the way to the edge of the tool.

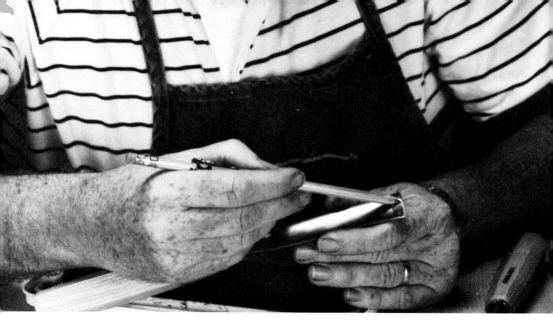

The pencil is pointing to the sharpened edge.

The pencil shows the angle of the blade leading to cutting edge.

Test the edge for sharpness on your thumb nail. If the blade catches and does not slide across the nail it is sharp enough.

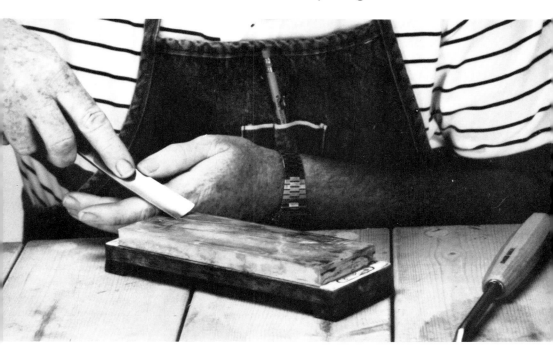

Begin to hone the blade on a finer 8000 grit water stone.

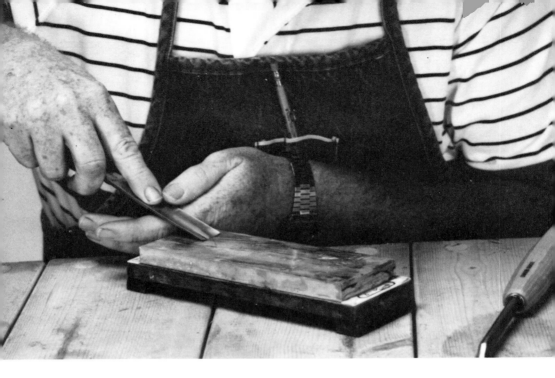

Hold the blade at the same angle as when sharpening.

Rotate along the edge of the blade.

Rub the compound on leather.

Apply the compound only to the area where it will be used.

Again rotating the blade, rub it on the leather.

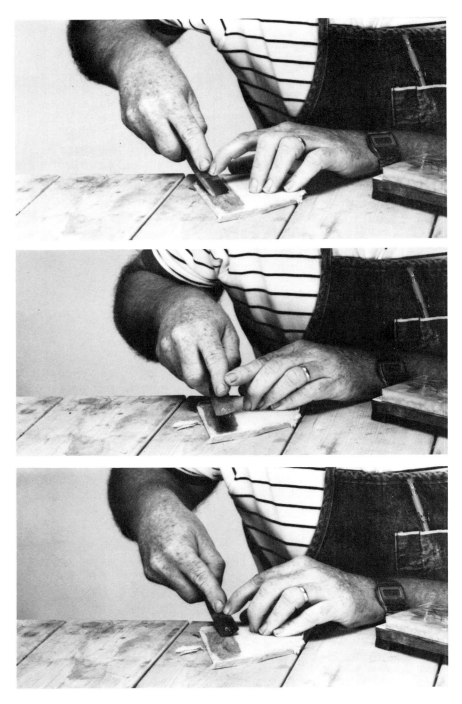

Continue to rotate the blade on the leather until there is a mirror finish along the blade.

A folded piece of leather rubbed with compound is used to polish the inside of the gouge.

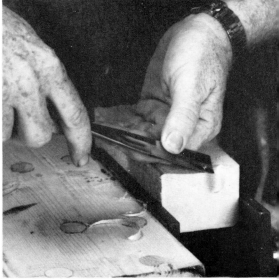

Check the sharpness on a piece of wood.

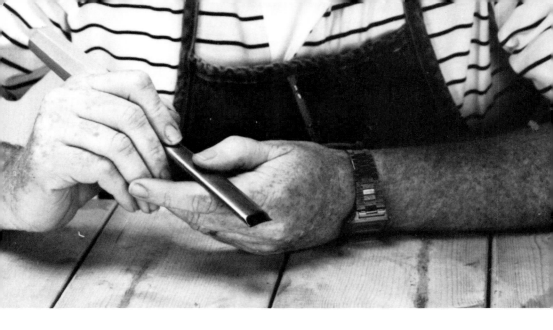

The mirror finish blade edge.

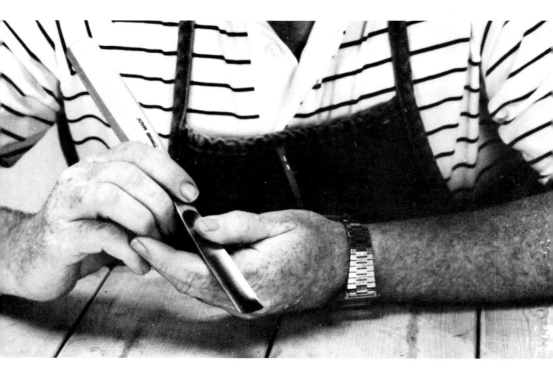

The polished underside of the blade.

Small Gouges

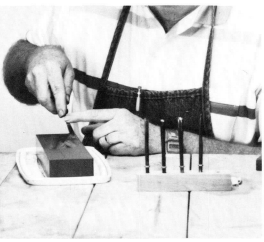 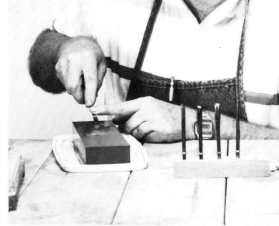

Small gouges sharpen just like larger gouges. Begin with an 800 grit water stone in the corner closest to the body.

Push the tool across the stone away from the body.

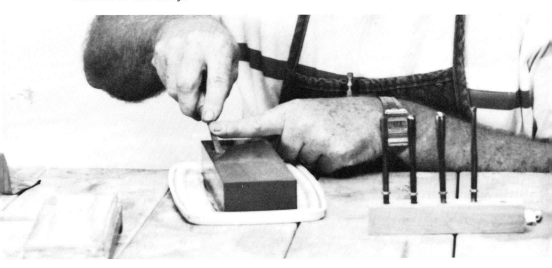

Rotate the edge from one side to the other as it is pushed along the sharpening stone at a 20-25° angle.

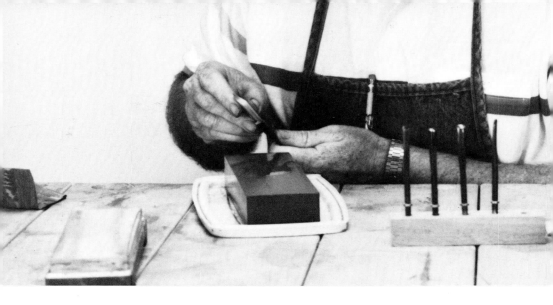

Use an appropriately shaped slip stone to sharpen the inside of the tool.

Hone and polish the tool on an 8000 grit stone and leather with fine grit compound. Use the same rolling motion for each step with the sharpening stone, honing stone and leather, always maintaining a 20-25° angle.

A folded piece of leather rubbed with compound is used to polish the inside edge.

This same process can be repeated for any of the gouges.

Use the same rolling motion at a 20-25° angle.

Be sure the slip stone is the correct shape for the tool being sharpened.

The marks on the 8000 grit stone indicate the direction the tool is taking as it is pushed and pulled across the surface.

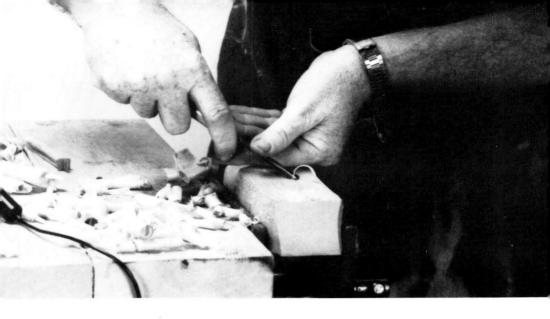

Check the blade on a block of wood.

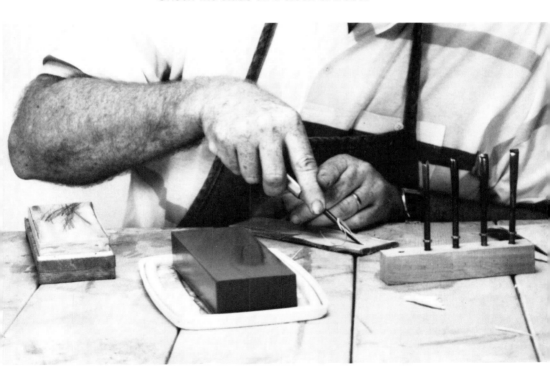

For a V gouge, cut a channel in a piece of leather.

Rub the channel with compound.

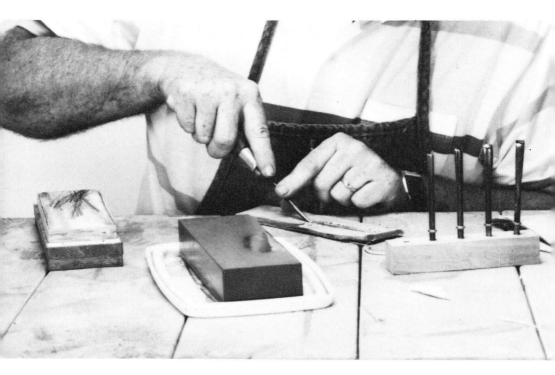

Pull the V gouge along the channel to hone the edge.

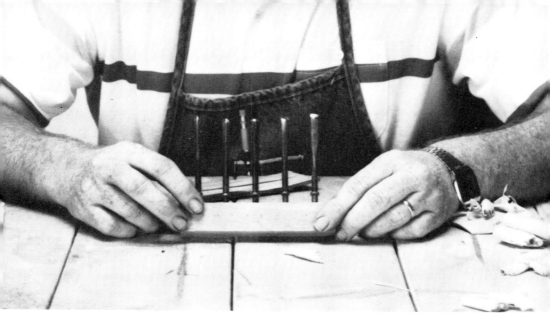

The sharpened set of small gouges.

Veiner

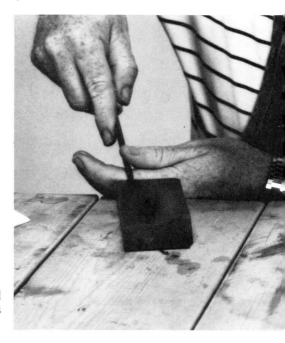

Using an Arkansas stone with oil lubricant, rotate the veiner across the stone, in a side to side motion.

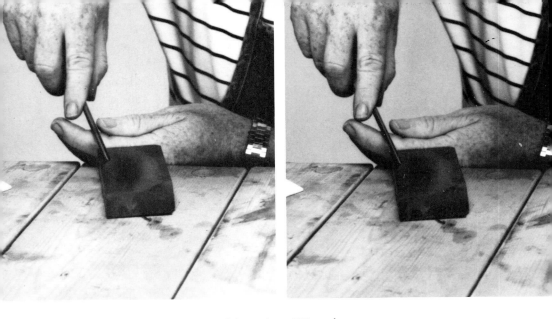

Maintain a 25° angle.

Hone the tool on a finer grit Arkansas stone also lubricated with oil.

Use the same rotating motion across the stone.

Hone the inside edge with a slip stone.

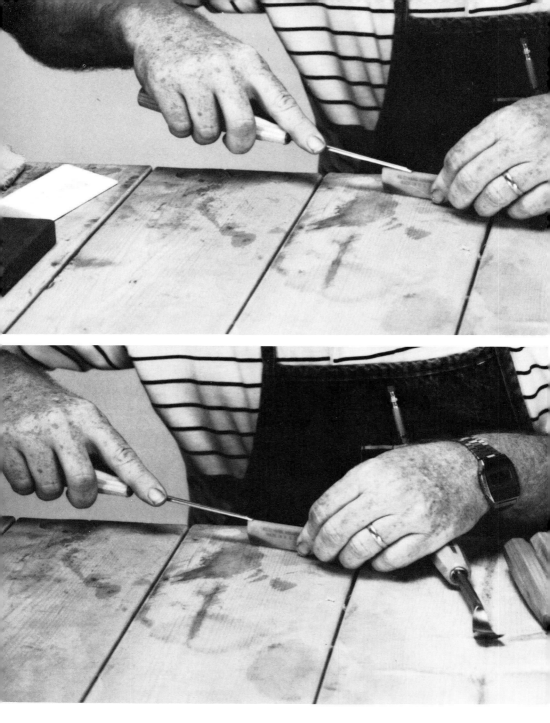

Pull the inside edge along the slip stone to further hone the edge.

Continue the honing process on leather with compound.

Use the same pulling motion as on the slip stone.

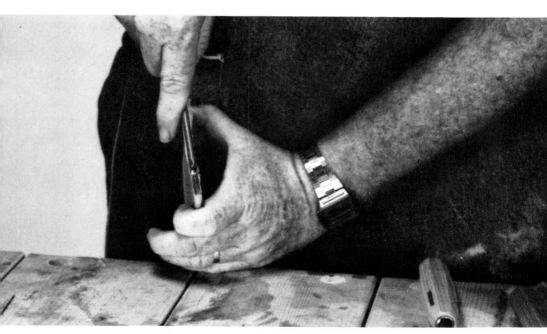

Further hone the inside of the veiner along the edge of a piece of leather.

Test for sharpness on a block of wood.

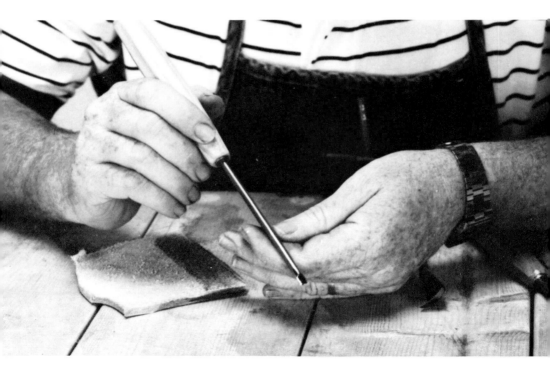

The finished edge.

Parting Tool #12

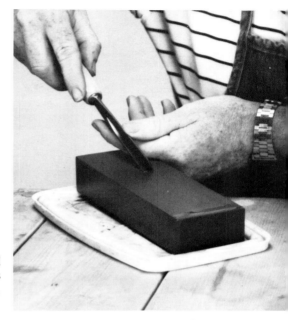

A parting tool should be treated like two straight skews or chisels joined together in a V shape. Begin at a 25-30° angle.

Pull the tool flat along one side of the stone.

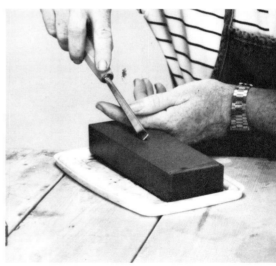

Repeat process on the other side of the tool.

Examples of slip stones used to sharpen special shape tools.

Sharpen inside of parting tool with slip stone which has shape closest to that of the tool.

Continue to polish the tool on finer grit 8000 stone.

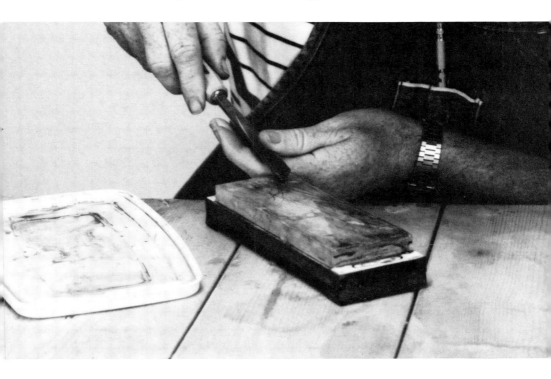

Use same pulling method on each side of the tool.

Keep proper angle held steady by guiding hand.

After rubbing compound on leather begin to polish the edges.

Hone the point.

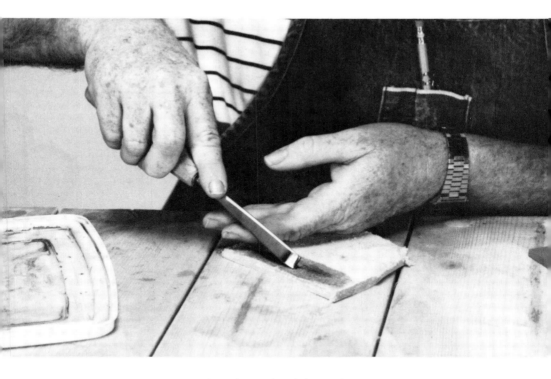

Hone the other side of the tool.

Cut a piece of leather to fit the tool.

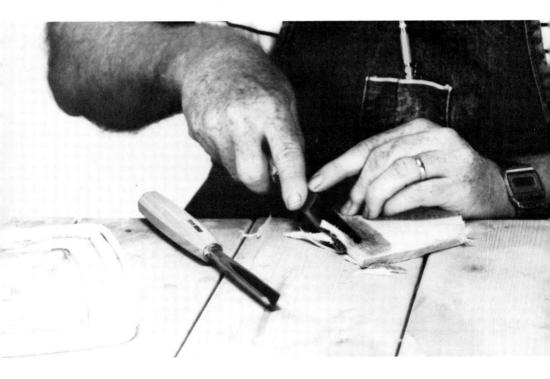

Trim both sides of the leather's edge until the desired shape is obtained.

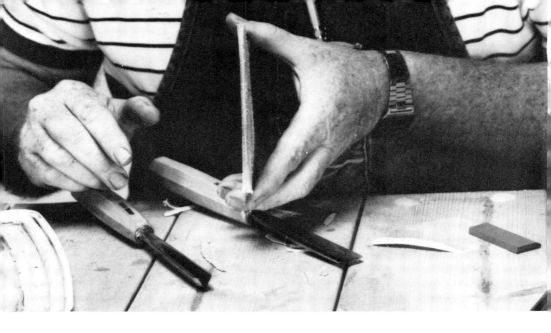

The edge should be V-shaped when finished.

Use this leather V to polish the inside edge of the tool.

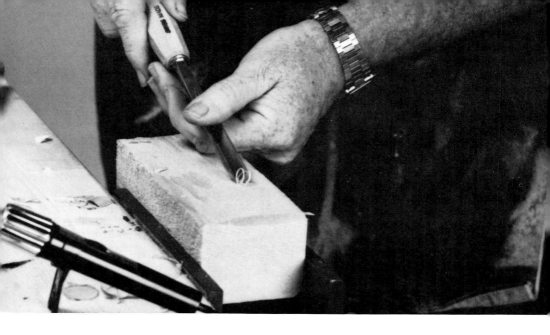

The sharpened tool should be able to make small curls of wood.

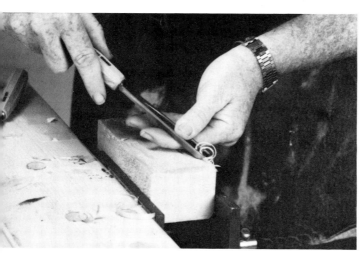

Carving should be possible in any direction.

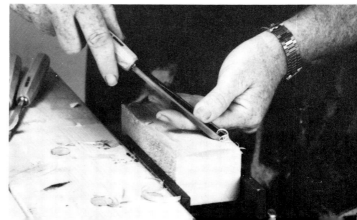

The sharpened parting tool.

Spoon Gouges

Spoon gouges are shaped similar to the typical table spoon and are used where a straight blade is not practical. Examples of spoon gouges.

Use black ink to mark the end of the bevel. This shows the cutting edge and where to sharpen.

Begin to sharpen along the beveled edge of the gouge at a 25-30° angle.

Rotate edge along the water stone.

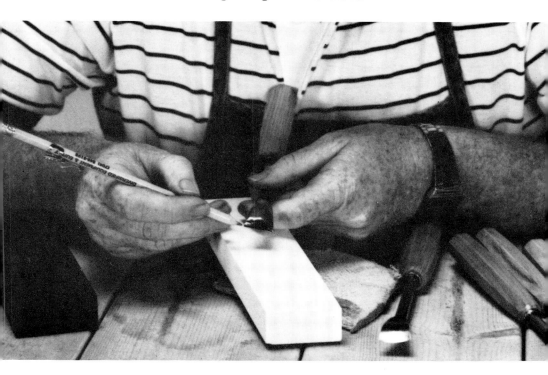

As sharpening progresses, notice how the black marks begin to wear off the edge.

More of the black removed from the edge.

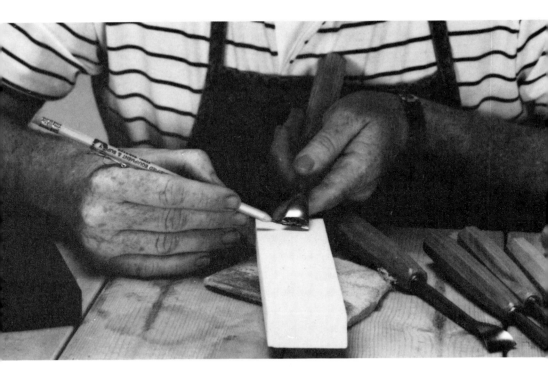

Check the edge.

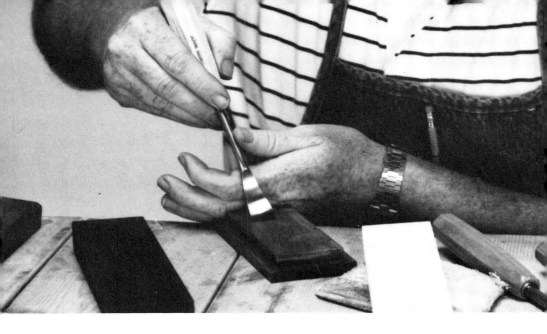

Continue sharpening if needed.

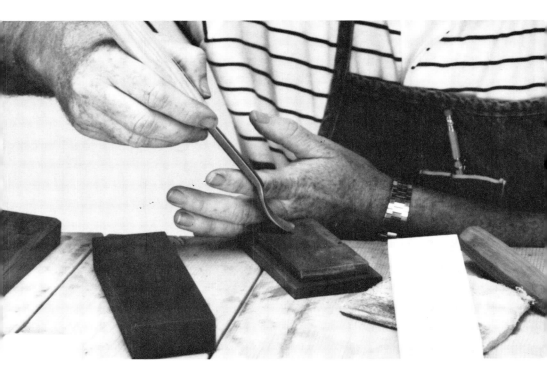

Keep rotating blade on a 25-30° angle.

Hone the edge on leather.

Use the same motion as in the sharpening process. Do not overhone the edge and roll it over which creates a dull tool again.

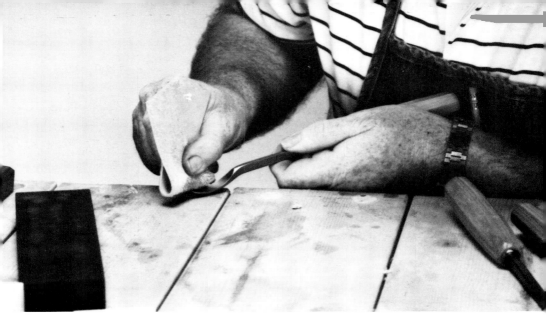

Hone the inside edge with a piece of folded leather.

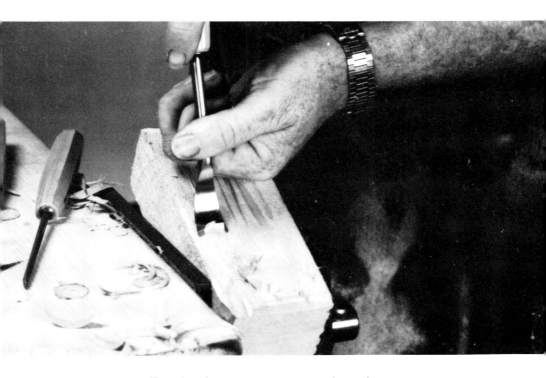

Test for sharpness on a piece of wood.

The finished mirror edge.

The other spoon gouge #25, is sharpened on an Arkansas stone with honing oil lubricant.

The motion is the same as with the prior spoon gouge.

Be careful not to roll over the edges or cut them off.

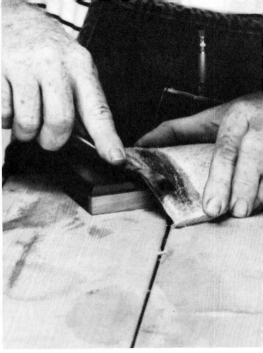

Hone on a piece of slightly bent leather.

Use the same rotating manner on the leather. Once this technique is mastered, honing can be done on a polishing wheel.

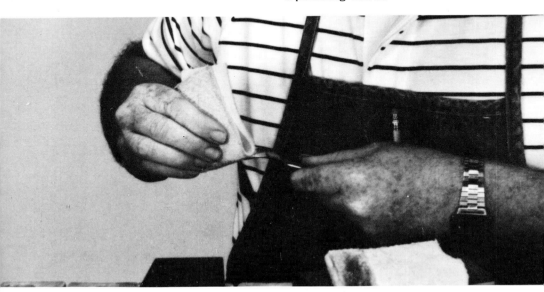

Use a small piece of leather to finish honing the edge.

Palm Gouges

 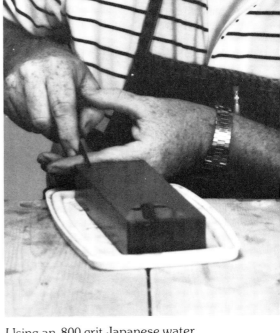

Palm gouges are small carving tools made to be held in the palm of the hand. They are used primarily for detail work.

Using an 800 grit Japanese water stone, the procedure is the same as for a larger gouge, use a 25-30° angle.

A slip stone sharpens the inside of the blade.

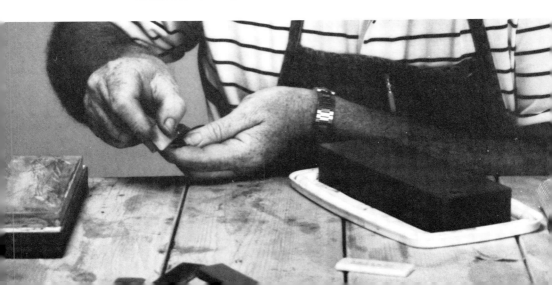

Hone the gouge on leather or the wheel, whichever is preferred.

When sharpening a V-tool, be careful to maintain the V in the center. If it is pushed to one side the sharpening process must be started over again. Refer to the instructions for sharpening a parting tool.

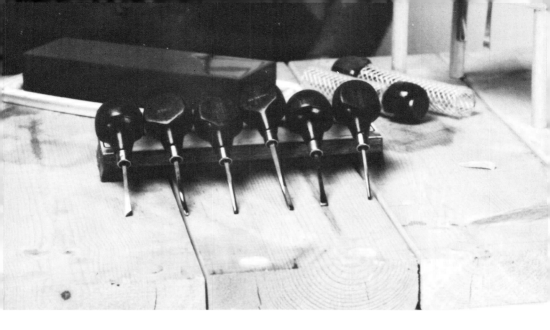

Variety of palm gouges. Store in small sections of garden hose to protect the blades.

Carver's Hooks

Carver's hooks come in two sizes, 1⅞" and 2⅜". Both hooks allows you to sharpen both sides of the hook with the same stone. The procedure for sharpening the hooks is the same for each one. Caution should be used when polishing the hooks on the wheel as the curved edges have a tendency to catch on the fabric of the polishing wheel.

Sharpen the 1⅞" hook with a round slip stone, called a carburndum stone, pushing the stone toward the edges of the tool. Sharpen toward the outside edges.

Wrap a piece of leather around the slip stone and using the same motions, begin to hone and polish the edges.

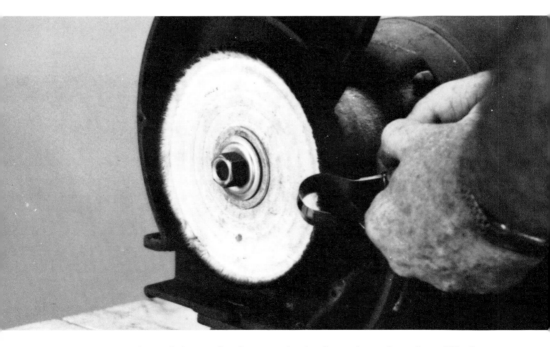

Jim uses the polishing wheel to put the final touch on the edges. Work back and forth between the leather and the wheel until the mirror finish edge is achieved.

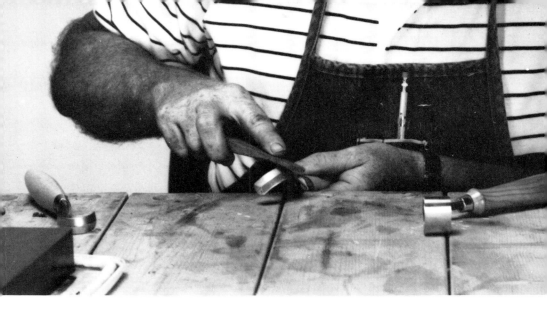

Using a flat slip stone, sharpen the 2⅜" hook, pulling the stone from the center of the blade out toward and off the edges.

Switch to a 4000 grit water slip stone as the blade becomes sharp.

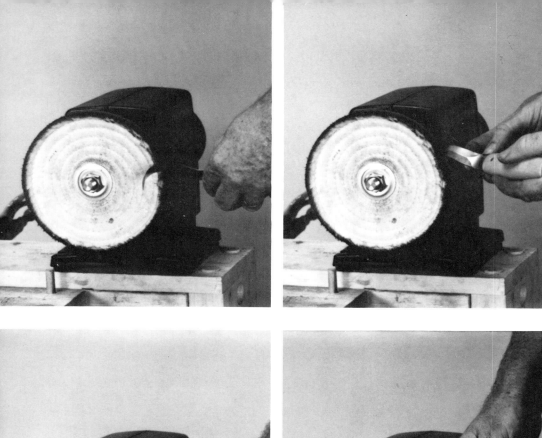

Polish the outside of the hook on the polishing wheel, then the inside of the hook. Hold the hooks tightly because the curved edge may cause them to grab at the wheel. Work back and forth between the leather and the wheel.

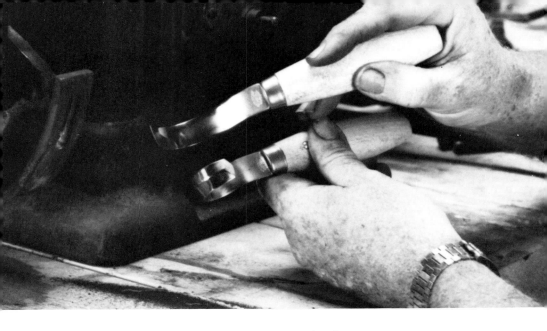

The sharpened carvers hook.

Scorp

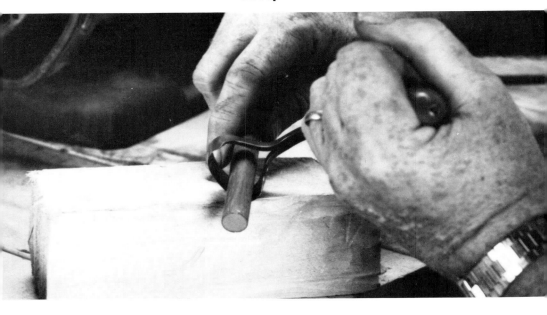

Sharpen the scorp using a carburndum stone. Push it from the inside toward the outside edge. Hone with a piece of leather wrapped around the slip stone as was done for the carvers hooks..

Polish the scorp on a polishing wheel with compound.

The sharpened, honed and polished scorp.

Micro Tools

These special little tools are used for creating detail in carvings and in making caricatures. They are made for very light work done on the surface of the wood, where it is not necessary to apply much pressure. Only a fine grit stone and leather are used in the sharpening process. A course stone will remove too much metal from the fine and delicate edges of the tool. When the tools are new it is easier to sharpen and hone them. Once honed it is only a matter of maintaining them. It is much easier to maintain a sharp edge than to re-create one.

When beginning to sharpen micro tools, only use a 1000 grit stone. The tool being sharpened here is a skew. Lay the skew on the rock to see the factory ground edge.

Raise the skew lightly to a 20° angle for sharpening.

Drag the skew back across the stone toward yourself in a flat straight motion. The fine edge of the tool will cut into the stone quickly and can ruin the edge. The skew must be sharpened in a flat motion, no rocking, rolling or twisting.

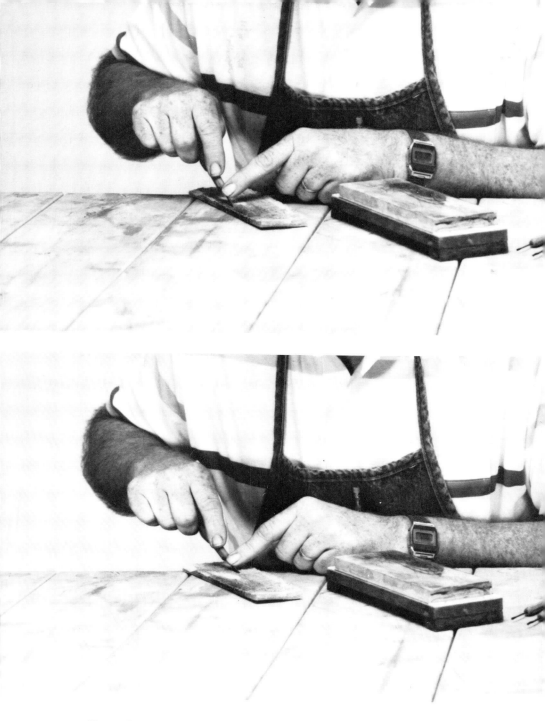

Hone the skew on leather using the same flat, even stroke.

To see the sharpening progress, check the micro skew through a magnifying glass. Look for a mirror edge.

Rotate round tools from side to side along a 1000 grit stone as shown in the instructions for sharpening gouges.

Roll on a 20-25° angle, being careful not to roll too far and go over the edges.

Sharpen the inside edge along a thin piece of leather, or the corner edge of a thicker edge.

Be sure to hold the same angle.

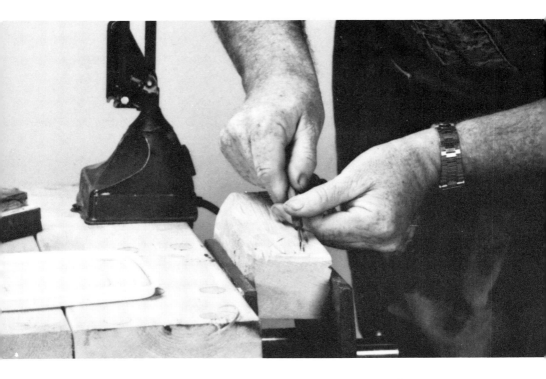

Check for sharpness on a piece of wood.

Cutting too deep with a tool not designed for it will cause the tool to dig too deeply into the wood and in some cases, break.

A V-tool is essentially two straight skews joined together at 20-25° angles. Sharpen one side with the same motion as sharpening a skew. Refer to the instructions for sharpening a parting tool.

Sharpen the other side, but do not overdo the radius and create a gouge from a V-tool. Maintain the V.

Hone on the flat leather, also like a skew.

Hone the inside surface along the corner edge of a piece of leather.

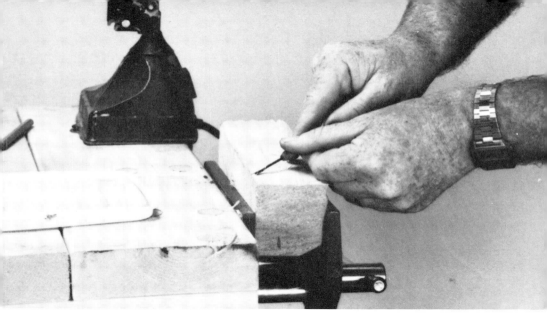

The V tool is sharp when it cuts easily and smoothly in shallow cuts across the grain.

Micro tools in their case.

Plane Iron

Two different devices for sharpening a plane iron are shown here. One uses the stone itself to stabilize the angle and the other uses the work table. Both work equally well and can be set to ensure the proper height and angle to use in sharpening. Instructions for the use of both come with the sharpeners when they are purchased. Remember that one side of a plane iron is beveled and one side is flat.

Remove plane iron from frog and put it in a sharpening guide.

Adjust the guide to allow for the dimension of the stone and/or the correct angle at which to sharpen.

Begin to sharpen on a perfectly flat   800 grit water stone.

Pull the blade along the stone toward your body. Hone the blade on an 8000 grit water stone with the same technique.

The plane iron sharpened to a mirror finish edge.

Test the plane for sharpness and flatness on a piece of wood.

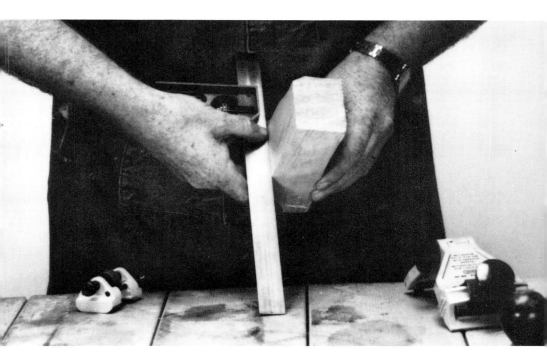

Properly sharpened, it should shave the wood easily, leaving a flat surface.

Inshaves

This tool is used to hollow out wood to make a dough bowl. Two inshaves are shown, one from the factory and one that has been customized. The reconstructed version has had the handles bent so the hands would not have to run across the wood as the tool is being pulled along.

Sharpening an inshave can be quickly and easily done on a belt sander, however if one is not available sharpening by hand is not a difficult procedure.

When a tool is purchased from the factory, check the blade for an uneven or crooked edge. To polish an inshave, only slip stones will be used because of the shape of the tool. A tool that dulls quickly has poor quality steel.

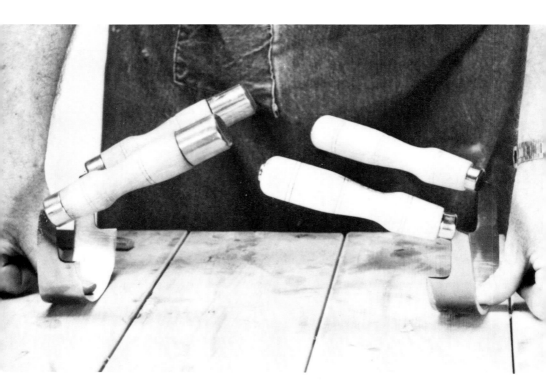

The reconstructed inshave on the left and the factory inshave on the right.

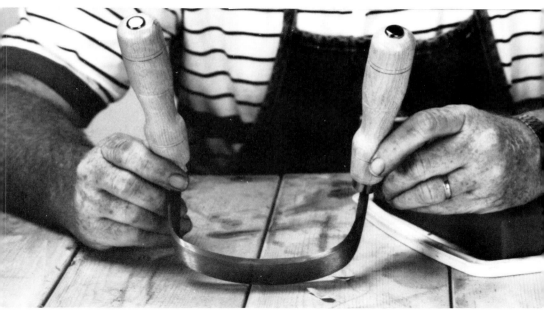

The factory inshave before it is sharpened.

Sharpen the outside edge of the inshave with a coarse slip stone, push the stone toward the handles.

Using an appropriate slip stone, sharpen the inside edge of the inshave pushing toward the handles. Try to maintain no more than a 10-15° angle.

With a finer slip stone, continue to sharpen the edge.

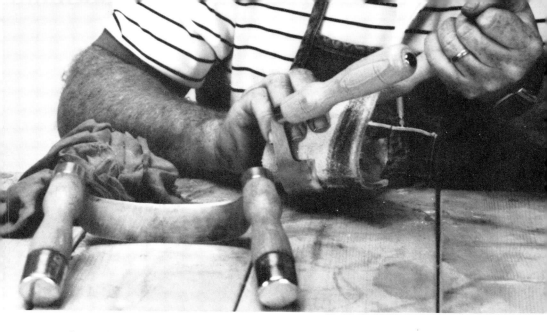

Once sharp, hone and polish the edge with leather and compound. The leather will gently remove the wire edge.

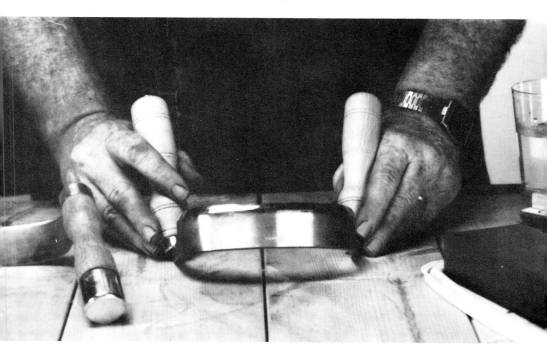

Finished mirror edge of inshave.

Sharpening Carving Knives

Draw knife

The draw knife also has a flat side and a beveled side. Large blades such as these take a particular amount of patience, but do not get discouraged, get dedicated. The results will be well worth the trouble.

A draw knife with the factory ground edge.

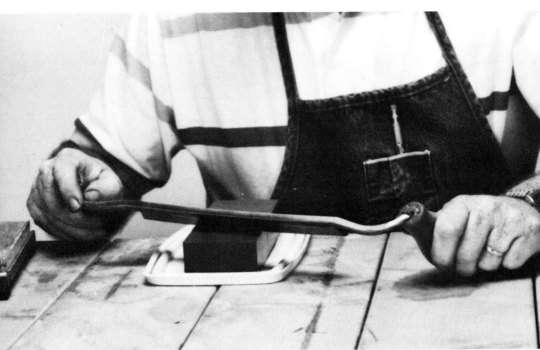

On a 25-30° angle, begin to sharpen the beveled side in a slow even motion working toward the body.

Continue along the edge of the blade. Use an 800 grit water stone.

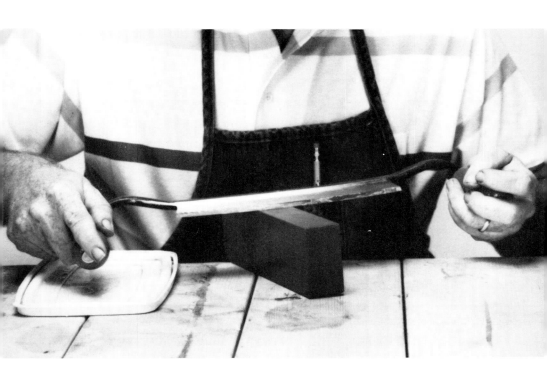

The flat side is sharpened flat on the stone, using the same motion.

Change to the 8000 grit water stone and begin to hone the edge, using the same motion as previously.

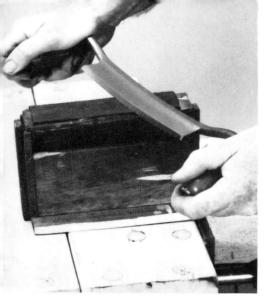

Test the sharpened edge on a piece of wood. You should be able to make onion skin-like shavings.

Buff out all the lines along the edge with a 4000 grit slip stone.

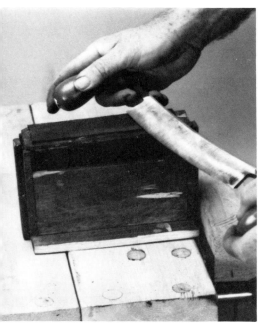

Strop the blade on the compound coated leather. Maintain a 25-30° angle. Hold the angle as on the water stones and keep a straight edge.

The sharpened draw knife with the mirror finish edge.

Carving Knife

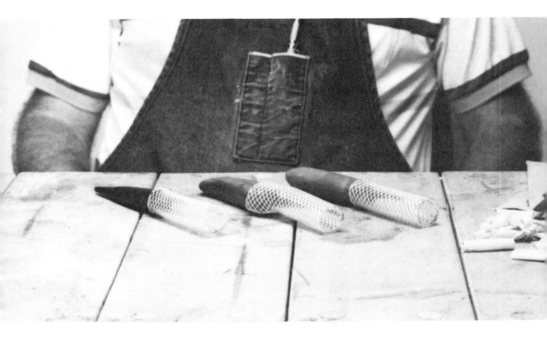

Pieces of garden hose are used to protect knife blades while not in use.

Using an 800 grit water stone, face the blade away and pick up the back of the blade creating a slight angle at the edge, 11-12°. Push the blade along the stone.

Turn the blade over and draw it back toward your body, across the stone. Sharpen both sides evenly.

Change to the 8000 grit water stone to further sharpen the blade and create the wire edge.

Use the same motion and angle as when sharpening the knife.

Keep checking the edge and do not over-hone, causing the blade to roll over and become dull again. Sharpen evenly on both sides.

The sharpened knife, ready for honing and polishing.

Using a leather block with the medium grit compound begin to hone the blade.

The motion of the blade is the same as when sharpening.

Put the final polish on the blade with a leather block covered with the most fine grit compound. If a wire edge appears again, carefully remove it through honing.

The sharpened, honed and polished blade.

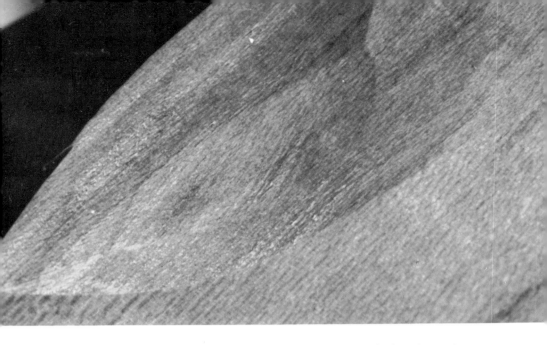

Fuzzy lines in a cut mean the knife is not sharp enough. Any fuzzy dust on a carving means a dull knife is being used. The cut should be clean.

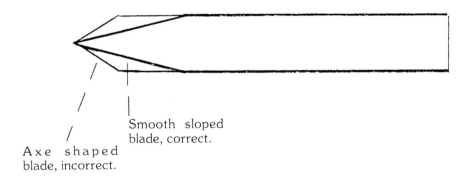

Axe shaped blade, incorrect.

Smooth sloped blade, correct.

A common mistake in sharpening a knife is to do so at too steep an angle, creating big shoulders on each side of the edge. It is quicker and easier to sharpen in this way, however it is wrong and will create an axe shaped blade. The big shoulders make it more difficult for carving because they will ride along the wood and hold the blade edge away from the wood. The edge may shave but not carve.

Warren Knives—small blades.

Begin to sharpen the blade with a turned up edge on an 800 grit water stone.

Be sure to sharpen the entire curve, taking care not to cut into the stone. Maintain a 20° angle.

Sharpen both sides of the blade evenly.

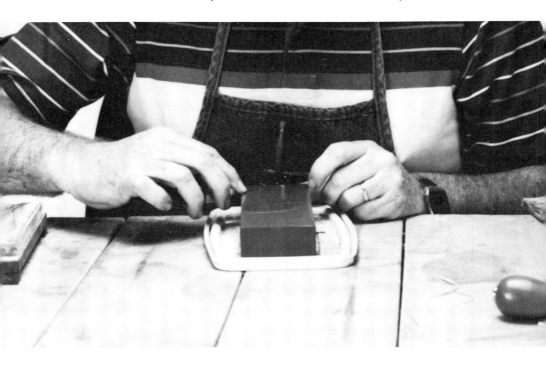

Push the blade away, then turn it over and pull it back toward you along the stone.

Sharpen until the wire edge is apparent and then change to the 8000 grit stone.

Use the same push and pull motion.

When ready, continue to hone and polish on the leather. Use the medium grit compound first.

As you progress, change to the fine grit compound and leather.

Sharpen the knife with a turned down blade in much the same way. Begin on the 800 grit stone.

Sharpen evenly on both sides, pushing and pulling the blade along the stone.

Progress to the 1000 grit stone.

Use the same motion, being sure to evenly cover the entire edge of the curved blade.

Hone using leather and medium grit compound.

Polish with the leather and fine grit compound.

The blades sharpened to a mirror edge.

Pocket Knife

A pocket knife differs from a wood carving knife in how it should be sharpened. The narrow edge of the carving knife will be too weak for a pocket knife. Also the pocket knife is naturally used for different purposes. The pocket knife should be held at a 20° angle, the more angle the stronger the edge will be. Pocket knives should always be sharpened by hand, never on a file or grinder.

When any knife comes from the factory it has shoulders shaped on the blade. These are removed when sharpening the blade so that a smooth blade is left down to the cutting edge. This ensures the correct angle for sharpening and a good clearance for cutting is achieved.

Begin sharpening the pocket knife on an 800 grit water stone. With the blade facing away push it along the wet stone.

Turn the blade the other direction and pull it toward your body across the surface of the stone until the knife is sharp. Sharpness can be tested by seeing if the edge of the knife will catch on the surface of your fingernail or if it just slides along. If it catches, it is sharp.

Repeat the process on a 1000 grit stone to further define and create the wire edge.

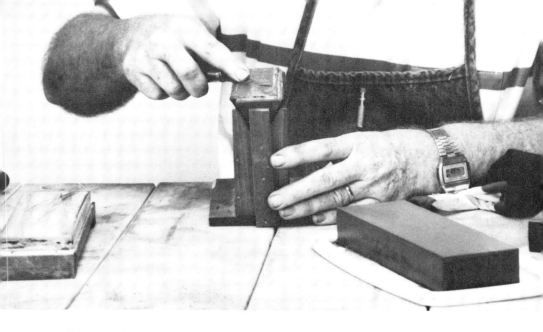

Begin to hone the blade on the leather with the most coarse grit compound.

Finish by polishing the blade with the leather having the finest compound.

The sharpened pocket knife.

Sharpening Kitchen Knives

Kitchen knives are used and abused daily. A few of the chief causes of abuse are; cutting meat in the frying pan, chipping ice, and opening cans. The primary rule to keep in mind is that a knife should always be used with a cutting board and should never be used as a tool. The knives illustrated are a 10″ butcher knife, a paring knife, a filet knife and a stainless steel fish knife.

Butcher Knife

This butcher knife is being sharpened on an 800 grit water stone. The back edge of the knife should be on the inside.

Begin at the tip of the blade and push the knife edge away along the stone.

To sharpen the other side of the blade, turn the knife over and repeat the same process pulling the blade back towards the body. Notice that the angle is steeper than when sharpening carving knives, about 20°.

Add water to the stone as needed to keep it well lubricated, and continue to sharpen both sides of the blade evenly.

Once the knife is sharp, change to the 1000 grit water stone to further refine the cutting edge.

Jim's left hand is used to steady the blade and apply slight pressure as needed while drawing the edge across the stone.

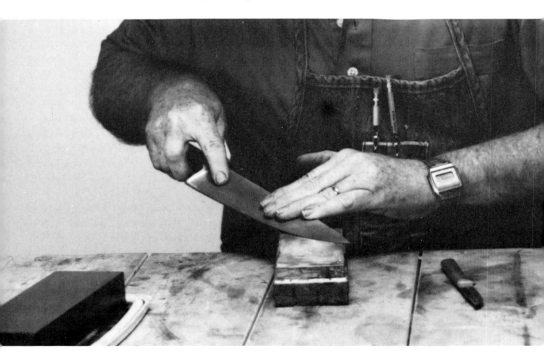

The motion of the knife is the same as that used with the 800 grit stone.

The final honing and polishing is done on the leather block.

Pull the blade toward you along the leather. Strop the entire edge to the tip.

Pushing the blade away along the leather, hone the reverse side of the blade.

Be sure to evenly run the blade along the leather. Jim removes the shoulders on his knife blades and gives them a smooth even slope.

Paring Knife

The paring knife needs a thin edge for slicing and peeling. Pull the knife edge along the sharpening stone at a 10°-12° angle.

Pull the knife edge along the stone to sharpen the other side. The shoulders of the paring knife have been removed to make a smoother surface.

The paring knife is stropped on leather in the final step. Be sure the very point is sharp so it will pierce easily for peeling. The movement of the knife along the leather is the same as pushing and pulling it along the sharpening stone.

Sharpen the filet knife on the 800 grit stone to start.

Change to the 1000 grit stone for final sharpening. Remember to follow through along the point and keep the angle consistent. Finally, give the knife a few "licks" along a piece of leather to polish the honed edge..

Sharpening the fish knife is the same procedure used for the other kitchen knives. When sharpening a long blade there may be a slight bend in the blade because of the pressure applied to it while pushing and pulling it along the sharpening stone. As long as the angle of the blade is maintained the bend is not a problem.

Reconditioning
Tools and Stones

Reconditioning and Sharpening a Chisel

Reconditioning is necessary for a badly worn blade or one that is no longer fit just to sharpen. Usually reconditioning is done on a grinding wheel. Keep in mind—the finer the grit the more heat it will create and transfer to the tool. If metal is overheated it will lose it's temper creating a soft edge to the blade. Water should always be close by to dip the tool into, keeping the temperature down. When using a grinding wheel for the first time, have someone who is experienced with the wheel nearby if help should be needed.

Hold the chisel lightly against the grinding wheel.

Applying only slight pressure while moving the cutting edge along the wheel, keep the correct angle in mind, 25-30°. Take your time.

Once a new edge has been established, switch to a sharpening stone. Rotate the edge from one side to the other.

Maintain the 25-30° angle.

Completely sharpen the edge.

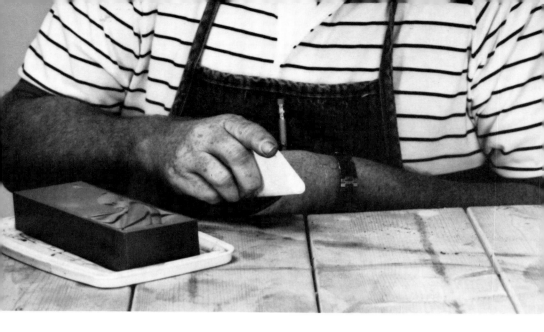

Use a slip stone to remove the wire edge created while sharpening. This must be removed prior to carving or the blade will be damaged.

Begin to hone the blade on the finer 8000 grit water stone.

Use the same rotating process.

Be sure to evenly hone the entire length of the blade edge.

On a polishing wheel, polish the blade with a compound covered leather wheel.

Polish the inside as well as the outside edge.

Test the finished new blade on a block of wood. A properly sharpened edge cannot be seen when looking straight into the blade because there is no surface from which to reflect light.

Reconditioning Sharpening Stones

After a stone has been used repeatedly for sharpening, the surface will become warped and uneven. When this occurs it is time to recondition the stone and bring it back to its original flat surface. Water stones wear down more quickly than oil stones, however both will need periodic reconditioning. Oil stones are more difficult to resurface and take more time than water stones. The procedure for both is the same.

To recondition a stone find a perfectly flat surface, preferably a piece of glass. Place a piece of 320 grit sandpaper on top of the glass and wet the coarse surface a little with water.

Rub the stone across the sandpaper creating a new flat surface on the stone.

Knife Making

The advantage of making your own knife is that it can be shaped and customized completely to your specific needs. The blade can be as short or long, wide or narrow depending on the job it is intended to do. The handle can be plain, ornate, thick or thin to fit the grip of the user. Jim makes carving knives for his customers with a square unshaped handle. That way each individual can carve the handle into the shape that best suits them.

The truth is, however, that it is easier and cheaper to buy a knife than to make one. Yet, a purchased knife does not provide the sense of pride and satisfaction that comes from having made the knife you carve with. For Jim Watson, knife making is a task he welcomes and enjoys. But he does feel that someone without *desire, dedication* and *determination* should think twice before planning to take on the task of knife making. It is time consuming and requires practice and patience, the rewards, however, are plentiful.

Here we will show how to make three different knives using spring steel, 01 steel and a straight razor. 01 steel is available in various sizes, both in flat and round pieces. The 01 steel used in this example is ⅜" flat ground steel, 1/16" thick. Spring steel is used to make springs and the tines of a hay rake. It is 1/32" thick. The straight razor is the traditional shape and was tempered before it was shaped into a razor so it will not require the heating process.

Tempering

The purpose of tempering is to make hardened steel less brittle and eliminate the structural problems caused by sudden cooling during quenching. The tempering process involves heating the steel to a specified temperature and then cooling it.

Heating steel rearranges the molecules. Both tempering and drawing back achieve this change of the molecules and in turn effects the hardness of the steel. The method presented here for tempering steel is one of many. Untempered steel is not hard enough to hold an edge and stay sharp. On the other hand, once steel is tempered and heated again incorrectly, the temper will be ruined as well as the strength of the steel.

There are many means of heating steel; for our purposes, we will use an acetylene torch. Tempering is a two-fold heating process. The first heating brings the steel to a bright cherry red color. It is then quenched or cooled in oil. Finally, it is heated again to a pre-determined color or temperature depending upon how hard the steel needs to be.

In the following examples the spring steel will need to be heated to a higher temperature than the 01 steel because of the difference in the types of steel and the uses for which they are intended.

During the tempering process, steel can be heated to a number of levels depending upon the desired strength. Below are temperatures and corresponding colors relevant to plain carbon steel.

430° F . . . very pale yellow	510° F . . . spotted red-brown
440° F . . . light yellow	520° F . . . brown-purple
450° F . . . pale straw-yellow	530° F . . . light purple
460° F . . . straw-yellow	540° F . . . full purple
470° F . . . deep straw-yellow	550° F . . . dark purple
480° F . . . dark yellow	560° F . . . full blue
490° F . . . yellow-brown	570° F . . . dark blue
500° F . . . brown-yellow	640° F . . . light blue

It takes considerable practice to properly temper a piece of steel. As Jim said, "Learning to temper is like learning to swim, anyone can tell you how to do it but you really won't learn until you jump in the water."

A primary reason for the majority of defects caused during the heating process is uneven heating. "Cracks of a circular form, from the corners or edges of a tool, indicate uneven heating and hardening. Cracks of a vertical nature and dark-colored fissures indicate that the steel has been burned and should be put on the scrap heap. Tools which have hard and soft places have been either unevenly heated, unevenly cooled or 'soaked', a term used to indicate prolonged heating." (Machinist Handbook)

The scales seen on the surface of hardened steel are caused by contact of heated steel with oxygen. The quenching bath removes heat from the steel at a rate faster than the critical cooling rate. In general, the more rapid the rate of heat extraction above the cooling rate, the higher the resulting hardness will be. Various kinds of quenching baths are used, depending upon the type of work the steel is to be used for.

The quenching bath used in the examples here is oil Oil is popular because of its ability to produce consistent results of hardness, toughness and freedom from warpage in standard types of steel. Various kinds of oil can be used. Mineral oils are widely used because they have good quenching characteristics, chemical stability, no offensive odor and are economical. Also, Linseed oil is very popular. Jim has found that Linseed works best. Put the oil in a container that is large enough to dip the entire piece of steel, usually about one pint of oil will be enough for one knife.

Oil cools at a rate fast enough for alloy steel yet slower than water. Different oils have different cooling rates which can vary through the initial and final stages of the quenching process. Faster cooling in the first stages and slower cooling at lower temperatures is better because there is less danger of cracking the steel. If you are going to note the temperature of the quenching oil the most efficient range is from 90 to 140 degrees F.

Tools

It is very important to be experienced or to have someone with experience available when working with an oxygen tank and acetylene torch. Oxygen, if improperly handled, can react like a torpedo and acetylene can blow up. Both are very dangerous and should be handled cautiously.

The same should be said for any power tool. The potential for an accident is strong and someone not familiar with power tools should seek the assistance of someone who will teach the necessary skills and techniques to use these tools safely.

To make your own knife, very few tools are needed. A grinding wheel and bench grinder are important and necessary tools. Also needed are sharpening stones, a piece of leather, compounds, a skew or gouge, a hack saw, an acetylene torch, oxygen tank, and quenching oil.

There are several types of wood that can be used to make a knife handle. In these examples walnut is being used. Cocabola wood is a good strong wood, also osage wood and purple heart are decorative woods that work well as handles.

Spring Steel Knife

The spring steel knife is made to use for detail and surface carving. This steel does not have the strength to withstand the pressure from deep or heavy carving. Spring steel must be tempered before it is ready to shape into a knife blade. This means it will be heated to a full blue color, roughly 560° F, to achieve the correct molecular structure to make it suitable for a carving knife.

Begin with a length of spring steel.

Place the steel in a vice and saw off the amount needed. Allow for the exposed section of steel as well as that secured inside the handle.

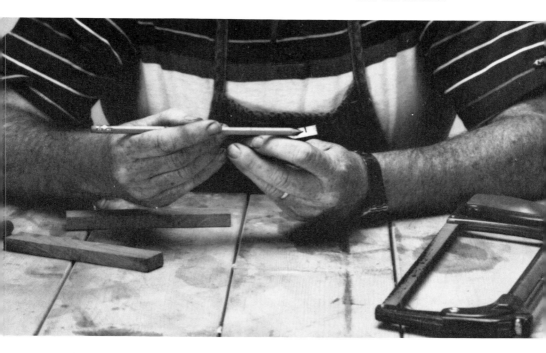

Close to the end of the piece make a second cut with the saw which will act as a heat sink during the tempering process.

This cut breaks the flow of heat into the plyers being held while the steel is heated. When the blade is put into the handle this cut will no longer be visible. This heating procedure must be done very carefully. Over heating will cause the steel to become brittle and break off.

Using an acetylene torch, heat the steel to a cherry red. This color should be achieved on the full length of the steel and it should be a good uniform color. As the color appears in one part of the steel, chase it along the entire length keeping it consistent.

Once the cherry red has been obtained, let the color dull slightly and then quench the steel in oil. Drop the steel straight into the oil, do not stir it around. You want uniform coolness and stirring will create uneven air pockets.

When the steel is removed from the quenching oil it should have scales on it and it will be extremely hard. It is actually too hard to do anything with.

When the steel is cool enough to handle, the scales can be wiped off on a rag. At this stage the steel is too hard to sharpen on a stone. If no scales are apparent on the steel it was not heated enough. Sand off the oxidation so the color will show up while drawing it back.

To make the steel possible to sharpen, the temper must be drawn back through a second heating. The color of the steel will indicate the hardness. A straw color means too hard to sharpen, purple is better but still too hard, blue is the desired color (54-57 rockwell hardness) for sharpening. Sand off the oxidation so the color will show up while drawing it back.

Drawing it back will make the steel softer so it can be worked; soft enough to work yet hard enough to hold an edge.

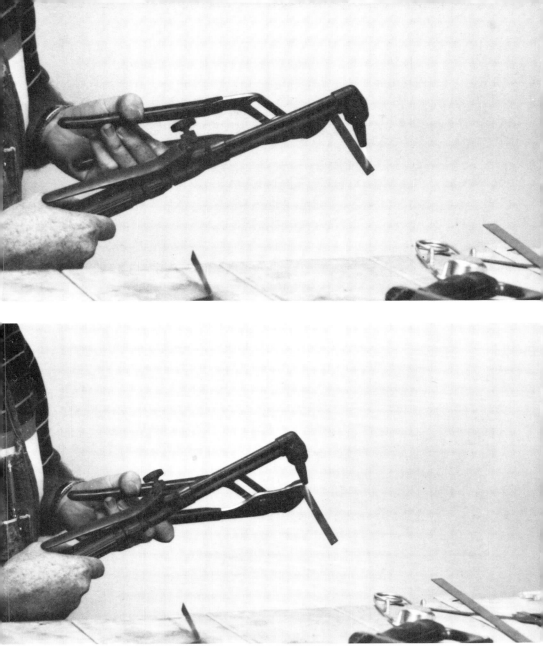

Heat the steel in the same way as before. It should be an even blue color along the full length of the steel. Once the draw back is completed, the steel should be allowed to air cool. The heating and draw back procedure will take practice to get the desired results. Do not get discouraged, once achieved the results will be well worth the effort.

The steel should now be tested to see if, when bent, it springs back into shape. If it does not spring back the procedure must be started over with the cherry red stage and carried all the way through the draw back stage again.

Now the steel is ready to be ground into the blade shape used to carve.

First, break off the heat sink and decide on the blade shape.

If the steel is over-heated during the grinding process, it will be ruined. Any red or purple color seen on the steel while grinding means it is too hot. Therefore, use of a wet wheel which constantly revolves through water makes it easier to keep the temperature constant and cool enough.

In the picture above, I show two examples of what NOT to do. DO NOT pour water on your wheel because you may electrocute yourself. Also, always hold the knife with two hands.

Grind the back of the blade and start to make the point. Keep dipping the blade in water to cool it as needed. The blade should not be too hot to touch. Hold the blade right against the tool rest on the grinder. The grinder shapes the edge of the blade.

The beginning stages of the carved knife.

The belt sander is used to speed up the process. Again, be careful not to overheat the steel. The belt sander thins the steel and shapes the flat surfaces. Do not create shoulders on the side of the blade.

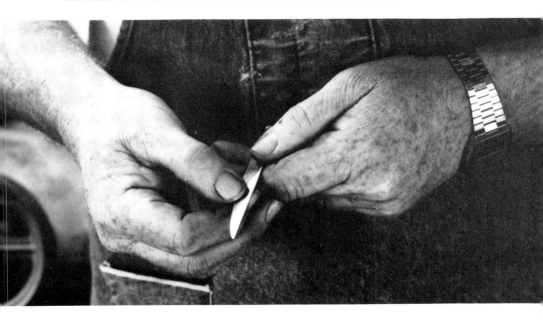

Be sure of the desired length of the blade and the shape you are trying to achieve. There should be enough steel for the handle to fit securely around.

While sanding and grinding, keep looking at the cutting edge. The flat surfaces must slope at the same angle toward the cutting edge.

Smooth the gradual slope of the flat surface of the knife toward the cutting edge.

The finished knife blade compared with the original piece of steel.

In the shank of the steel, grind a notch to be used to secure the blade to the wooden handle. This is done on an ordinary 36 grit grinding wheel.

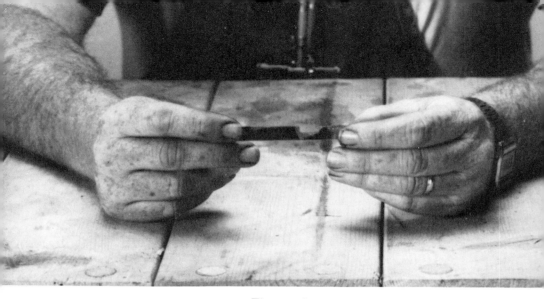

The notch.

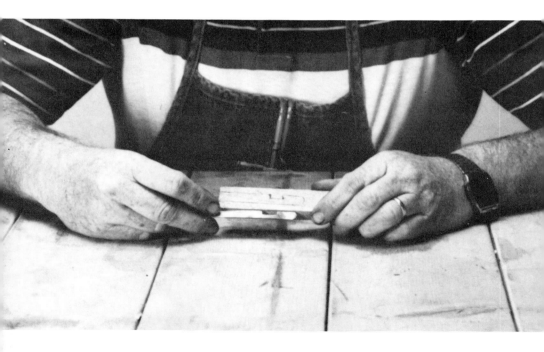

To begin making the handle, lay the steel on a block of wood and trace around its shape. The notch will act like a lock to keep the blade from sliding in and out of the handle. Leave the length of the knife blade exposed at one end with the desired length of the blade.

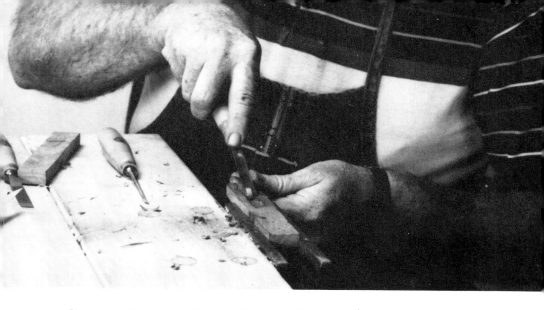

Carve out the width of the blade within the traced lines. Carve a little and then measure with the blade to be sure the carving is not too shallow or too deep. A router can be used for this step.

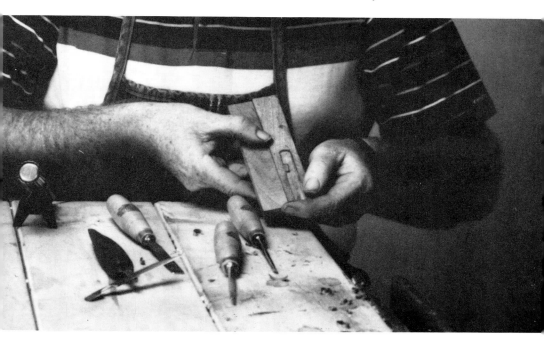

Be careful not to carve away the contour of the lock notch. Outline the design with a blade cut. A flat gouge will cut out the wood. Cutting into the handle will eliminate the need to put rivets in the handle.

153

Here two pieces of walnut will be used to make the handle.

Using 24 hour Epoxy Glue, apply some to the carved out area of the knife handle. Cover the rest of the inside of the handle with glue. Place the blade into position inside the handle.

Place the other piece of wood on top.

Press the wood pieces together in a vice to hold them tight and steady.
Be sure the blade is pointing down for safety purposes. Allow to set.

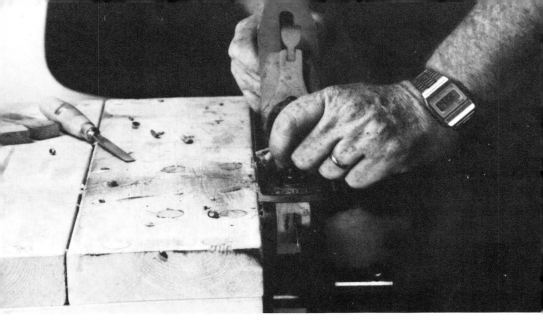

Wipe away any excess glue that may leak out the sides. It will be hard and brittle when it has dried and may have to be removed with a plane.

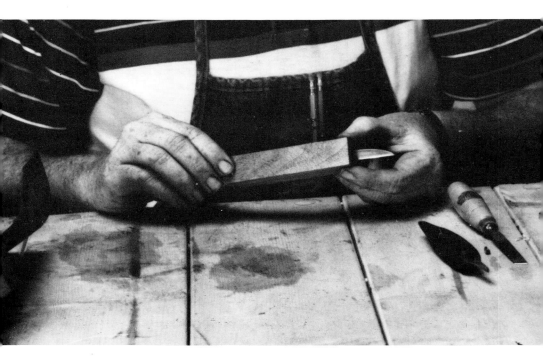

This example is being made for a standard size knife handle.

Leave the handle in a rough shape until after the blade has been sharpened.

The first step in shaping the outside of the handle is to draw the shape on the wood.

If lots of wood is being eliminated at the end of the handle, use a band saw to quickly remove it. Then rough out the shape of the handle on a belt sander. Narrow the wood and remove the square edges at the handle near the blade.

Remove enough wood so the handle is easier to hold. Sand off the hard edges. Be careful not to let the cutting edge make contact with the sander as it will damage the blade.

Once the handle has been rough shaped begin to sharpen the blade using an 800 grit stone. If the steel on the blade cuts away very easily the blade is too soft and did not reach the right temperature during the tempering process. A hard blade can be sharpened for a while before a change is noticeable. Maintain an 11-12° angle.

The sharpening process on a new blade takes a long time in comparison to sharpening a blade with an already established factory edge. Patience is important in this process. Be aware not to create big shoulders along the blade. Keep the blade smooth and tapered with both sides angled evenly. Note: The handle should also be in consistent shape with the blade and it's intended use. For example, a long thin blade for carving in small places requiring a lot of detail should have a narrow handle.

When enough metal has been removed from the blade, change to the 1000 grit stone and continue the sharpening process. Obtaining the right shape is not easy and you must be willing to work to achieve it.

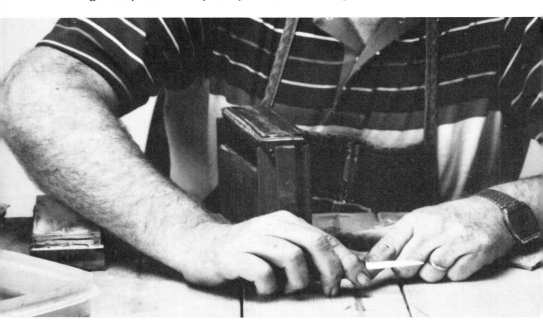

Examine the blade for high and low areas that need additional work. The following honing and polishing process will also show up areas that need more work.

As the blade becomes sharp, begin to hone it on the leather, looking for a progressively finer edge. Start with the most coarse grit compound.

Move on to the finer grit compound to smooth the edge and further increase the sharpness.

Among the final steps is polishing on the polishing wheel.

The final step is to hone again on the leather with a #3 lapping compound.

A finished, sharpened and polished knife compared to it's original form.

01 Steel Knife

    The knife made from 01 steel follows a very similar procedure to the process used in creating the knife from spring steel. It must be heated and tempered, however, it is drawn back to a color closer to straw (450° F) instead of the blue (560°) needed for the spring steel. If the 01 steel was drawn back to the blue color it would then be too soft to hold an edge. This type of steel is good to use for a standard sturdy carving knife.

    To begin the knife follow the same process used to temper the spring steel blade.

Begin with an appropriate length of steel and cut in the heat sink.

Holding the steel with pliers begin to heat the steel to a cherry red color using the acetalyne torch. Remember to follow the color along the entire length of the steel so the metal is heated evenly.

Once this step is achieved allow the color to dull slightly and then dip the steel in Linseed oil.

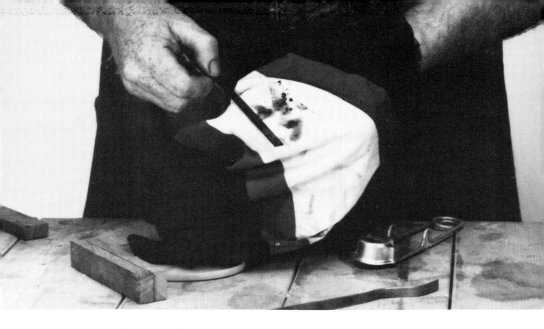

Scales will appear along the length of the steel once it has cooled. Wipe the scales off with a rag. The scales are an indication that the steel was heated to the correct temperature. Sand off the oxidation so the color will show up while drawing it back.

Using the acetalyne torch reheat the steel to draw back the temper. This steel will differ from that of the spring steel knife in that the color being looked for in reheating, is a straw color. In this case, straw is the desirable color for 01 steel to make a knife from. This is a 57-60 rockwell hardness.

Once the straw color has been achieved along the full length of the steel allow it to air cool. Now it is ready to be shaped into the actual blade. Begin to shape the blade on an 800 grit stone. This blade is being made with a turned down edge. Be sure the entire blade is kept in contact with the surface of the stone during the sharpening process.

Continue sharpening on the 8000 grit water stone.

The top of the blade is too curved so here we point out where to cut and trim the blade.

The shape of the top of the blade is changed on the grinding wheel. Wet the blade frequently so it does not get too hot and lose the qualities obtained during the tempering process.

The knife is now the proper shape for the type of detail carving it is intended for.

After grinding, the knife top edge is smoothed with a 1000 grit stone. The final honing and sharpening of the knife is done back and forth between the 8000 grit stone and the leather with compound. The end result is the razor edge and mirror finish.

When carving and shaping the knife handle be sure to carve with the grain and be careful not to nick the blade. Shape the handle so it is comfortable to use.

Sand the handle slightly to smooth the surface completely.

The handle can be finished with linseed oil, tung oil, varnish or polyurethane. Here it is rubbed with some linseed oil.

The two knives, one with a straight blade and one with a curved blade.

Straight Razor Knife

Making a knife from a straight razor is a less complex process because tempering is not needed. Care should be taken however not to overheat the steel during the shaping and sharpening and cause it to loose its temper.

Begin with a traditional straight razor with the handle removed.

Use the grinding wheel to remove the cutting edge of the razor because this edge is too thin and fragile to carve with. Grind down to the width of the knife you want, keeping in mind that the width of the back of the razor is too thick for a carving knife. Be careful not to overheat the blade of the knife, because it has already been tempered when made into a razor blade.

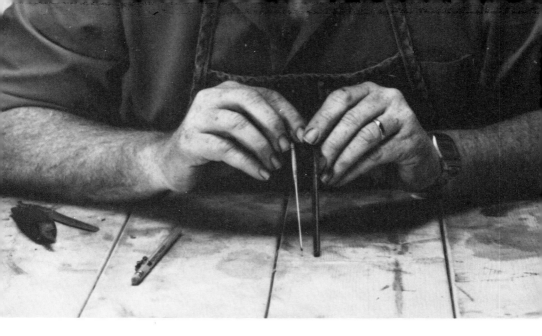

The width of the blade should be roughly 1/16".

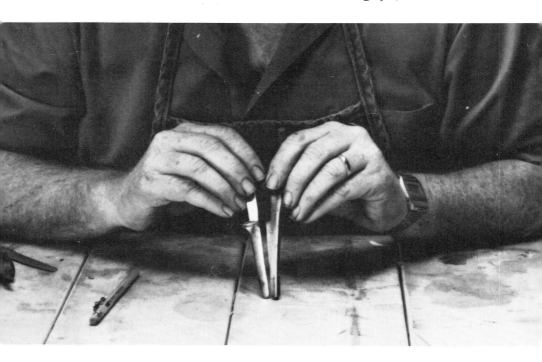

Grind the cutting edge on a belt sander. Using a grinder for this leaves marks on the blade, but it can be used.

Grind the back of the knife to the desired shape. Make the blade the length you need for the intended use.

Pieces of walnut have been cut on a table saw to be used as a handle.

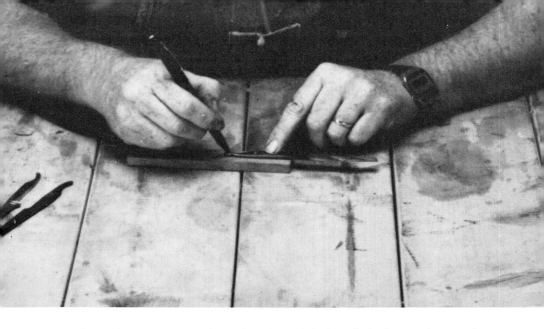

Draw the outline of the blade handle and the handle lock onto the wood chosen for the handle.

Put both sides of the handle together and draw the outside shape of the handle. Cut out the rough shape of the handle on a bandsaw.

Set the blade in the handle and epoxy the two sides together. Finish sanding and shaping the handle.

Sharpen the knife like any other knife. The completed straight razor knife.

About the Author

Jim Watson grew up in Stanley County, North Carolina. He has always been interested in how things are done the "old timey way." He learned blacksmithing and began making his own knives at an early age. Most recently, Jim has worked as a machinist for the past seven years. Prior to that he was in business for himself as a masonry contractor for ten years. The majority of his career has been in the brick laying business, roughly sixteen years.

Carving is a hobby for Jim and he has won numerous awards for carvings including ducks, horses and caricatures. Jim is very humble in his craft, he takes great pride in making his own knives and using his own tools including the table upon which he carves and sharpens. In addition to carving, Jim loves to hunt and fish, however he does not have much time for that anymore.

Jim is now the president of the Charlotte Woodcarvers Club and invites anybody in Charlotte on the third Sunday of the month to come by and visit him at the carving club.